You are the greatest gift I will ever know.
You're the place where love comes from.
I could tell you this every day and still not say
how much...

I love you, Mom.

~ K. D. Stevens

A Mother Is Love

Words of Love and Gratitude That Every Mom Will Cherish

Blue Mountain Press™

SPS Studios, Inc., Boulder, Colorado

Library of Congress Catalog Card Number: 2001005402
ISBN: 0-88396-610-7

ACKNOWLEDGMENTS appear on page 48.

Certain trademarks are used under license.

Manufactured in Thailand.
Fourth Printing: 2003

 This book is printed on recycled paper.

Library of Congress Cataloging-in-Publication Data

A mother is love : words of love and gratitude that every mom will cherish.
    p. cm.
  ISBN 0-88396-610-7 (hardcover : alk. paper)
  1. Mothers—Poetry. 2. Motherhood—Poetry. 3. Mother and child—Poetry. 4. American poetry—20th century.
  PS595.M64 M665 2001
  811'.540803520431—dc21

2001005402
CIP

Blue Mountain Arts, Inc.

P.O. Box 4549, Boulder, Colorado 80306

Contents

(Authors listed in order of first appearance)

My Mom

She is a person who
   believes in life's bright side.
I know, because she's helped me
   to find it many times.

She is someone who considers
   another's feelings first.
I know, because she's always
   cared for mine.

She is a friend who will stop
   everything else to listen,
to be a special source
   of understanding,
and to offer hope and help
   in any way she can.
I know, because she's always
   been a guiding light for me.

I know how wonderful my mom is,
   but what I wish for
is the perfect way to let her know
   how much she means to me.

I love you, Mom...
and just thinking of you
has the power to
   brighten up my day.

~ Barbara J. Hall

When I Look at You, I See a Mother's Love and So Much More

When I look at you, I see my life
through your eyes. I see the strength
you always offer me, the comfort you
continuously show me, the support
you provide me, and the magnitude
of the love that you unselfishly share.

I see the tears you shed when I cry,
the laughter you share when I laugh,
the hope you have for me when I feel
disillusioned, and the faith you have
in me when I face life's challenges.

I see the many sacrifices you have made
   and continue to make for me, the
   inspiration you are to me when I need
   direction, the devotion you show to me
   as a parent, and the encouragement
   you give me when I need a friend.

When I look at you and see my life
   through your eyes, I feel very loved,
   fortunate, and blessed.
Thank you for being all that you are to me
   and for being the best and more
      that a mother can be.

— Susan Hickman Sater

You Work So Hard
and Do So Much

You work so hard and do so much. And I know that you wonder sometimes — if anyone really appreciates the efforts you make on all those uphill climbs. Day in and day out, you make the world a better place to be. And the people who are lucky enough to be in your life are the ones who get to see...

You're a very wonderful person with a truly gifted touch. You go a million miles out of your way and you always do so much... to make sure that other lives are easier and filled with happiness. Your caring could never be taken for granted because the people you're close to are blessed... with someone who works at a job well done to bring smiles to the day.

You're a special person who deserves so much thanks.

— Jenn Davids

Mom,
I Want You to Know...

As a child, I took for granted that my life and my heart were safe in your hands. From the moment I was born, you loved me from the depths of your soul, no matter what I said or did. I didn't understand that as a child. I simply trusted you, and that in itself was probably the biggest compliment I could have given to you.

Now, as an adult, I realize what it means to truly love someone. And it warms my heart to know that no matter how I decide to live my life, what I succeed in, or how many times I fail, there is still one person in this world who will love me no matter what.

I know I don't tell you often enough, Mom, but I love you and I am grateful for the gift of your love.

~ April Adams

I Wish I Could
Do This for You, Mom

I wish I could make sure
   you always had the best –
like laughter, rainbows,
      butterflies, and health.
I wish I could take you anywhere
   you wanted to go
and treat you to waterfalls,
      rivers, forests, and mountaintops.
I wish I could make it possible for you
to do anything you ever dreamed of,
      even if just for a day.
I wish I could keep you from
      ever being hurt or sad,
and that all your troubles
      and problems would disappear.

I wish I could package up
all the memories that bring smiles to you
and have them handy for
   your immediate enjoyment.
I wish I could guarantee you peace of mind,
   contentment, faith, and strength,
as well as the constant ability
   to find joy in all the things
that sometimes go unnoticed.
I wish you moments to connect
   with other individuals
who are full of smiles and hugs to give away
and stories and laughter to share.
I wish you could always know
   how much you mean to me ~
because no matter what's going on in our lives,
you are loved and appreciated.

~ Barbara Cage

Thank You, Mother

I've been much too busy with other things in my life lately. I have taken your love for granted. Haven't been considerate enough. Haven't said "Thank you" enough. But I hope you will receive these words from me now...

Thank you for the sacrifices you have made for me. Thank you for all you've given me and all you've done for me.

I know there have been times that, had it not been for your unselfishness, my life would have been different: not as balanced, not as happy.

Thank you for giving me life. Thank you for your example. Thank you for being my mother. I wouldn't trade you even if I could. I love you so much.

— Donna Fargo

You Are Everything
a Mother Should Be

A mother should be
strong and guiding
understanding and giving
A mother should be
honest and forthright
confident and able
A mother should be
relaxed and soft
flexible and tolerant
But most of all
a mother should be a
loving woman
who is always there when needed
Mom, you are a rare
and wonderful woman
You are everything
that a mother should be
and more

— Susan Polis Schutz

I Don't Know
What I'd Do Without You!

Every time I see you, you smile your sweetest
smile and offer your kindest words. You
encourage me, inspire me, and remind me that
you love me and are always available —
whether I'm at my lowest point or filled
with joy and cheer. You are always behind
me absolutely.

Every time I see you, I am reminded of the
reasons I love you from the depths of my
heart. Without you, my spirit wouldn't know
the meaning of hope. Without you, where
would I be? Where would I go for comfort
and support? What would I do if I needed
your smile to show me that I am loved?

What would I do if I were feeling inspired
and needed to hear your words of faith —
or if I lost hope and needed to see your face
for a renewed sense of optimism and trust?
Without you... what would I do when
I wanted to share my happiest moments with
someone who truly understands and accepts
my deepest emotions? What would I do if
I needed someone who really loves me, cares
about my future, and understands my past?

What would I do if I didn't have you —
with your healing touch, your warmth and
comfort, and the sensitive way you have of
knowing just what I need at the moment?
Your wondrous, amazing love has always
been life's greatest gift to me!

~ Regina Hill

What Is a Mother's Love?

A mother's love is many things. She is a teacher and a friend, someone to guide you through right and wrong, someone to listen and understand.

She can comfort you like no other, holding you in her arms. She can fill your spirit with confidence and encourage your unsure heart.

She can bring a smile to your saddened face, wipe away your tears, love you regardless of the faults you have, and stand by you throughout the years.

A mother's love is many things, and one thing is quite sure: a mother's love is special, for no one can love like her.

— T. L. Nash

It Takes Someone Special
~ Just like You ~
to Raise a Child

To raise a child to be a person of worth requires a parent's caring use of so many special talents...

It requires someone who understands that a child's feelings change from day to day and each feeling needs love and nurturing.

It requires someone to receive those feelings as they would their own ~ handling each with honesty, gentleness, and care.

It takes a heart above the rest of the world to see a child's potential, to draw it out, to encourage their dreams, and to help with their plans.

To raise a child to be a person of worth takes someone who makes it a point to be that child's caring confidant.

It takes someone exactly like YOU to give a child so many reasons to believe they're a special someone on this earth... and your child will always appreciate your efforts.

~ Barbara J. Hall

You Have Made Me into the Person I Am Today

You're the most accomplished mother I know because
of what you've done in your lifetime.

You've taught me that an open heart moves mountains
and that great things come to those who love.

You've given me the ability to fit into this world and
the strength to challenge it.

You've shown me that happiness means being yourself
and being surrounded by those who do the same.

You've proven that sacrifice comes naturally when you
really, truly love someone.

You've taught me that being thoughtful is more
important than being thought of.

You've shared your talents with me and helped me
to develop my own.

You've gotten me started on the right foot and
   picked me up when I stumbled.
You've opened my eyes to the feelings of others
   and blinded me to their weaknesses.
You've helped me understand that the biggest
   mistakes can lead to the greatest rewards.
You've encouraged me when I was barely
   hanging on and given me insight that
   changed my course just in time.
You've not only given me life, you've given me
   perspective.
I'm a much better and wiser person because of
   you, and I thank you for a job well done.

~ Kari Kampakis

For You, Mom, Forever

You are my greatest inspiration.
You are my one ~ of ~ a ~ kind wonder.
You are someone who has touched my life with
    more caring than others could ever be capable of
    and more understanding than I will ever deserve.
You are an angel in my life.
You are a source of joy for my tomorrows.
You are a million memories from my past.
You are a positive influence on my days and
    on my dreams in a way that will always last.

You are the greatest gift I will ever know.
You're the place where love comes from.
I could tell you this every day and still not say
        how much...

       I love you, Mom.

~ K. D. Stevens

You are a remarkable woman
accomplishing so much as a
strong woman
in a man's world
strong but soft
strong but caring
strong but compassionate

You are a remarkable woman
accomplishing so much as a
giving woman
in a selfish world
giving to your friends
giving to your family
giving to everyone

You are a remarkable woman
who is also a remarkable mother
who is loved by so many people
whose lives you have touched
including mine

— Susan Polis Schutz

I Hope I've Been
the Kind of Child You
Always Wanted

So many memories have brought us
    close together over the years.
There was a time in my life when you
pulled me as close as you could
    to your heart,
because you felt I needed you.
Thank you — I did.
There were times in my life when
I needed your strength to walk
and your vision to see.
Thank you for being there for me.
Your honesty is the most valuable quality
I have gained from you over the years.
It has helped me to see who I am
and to help others accept themselves.
Thank you.

There are many other wonderful qualities
you have given to me through your love,
and I hope I have said "thank you"
      for them along the way.
Every day, I think about how fortunate
I am to have a mother as special as you.
If I could start my life over again,
I wouldn't change a thing —
except the number of times I've told you
      "I love you,"
for that can't be expressed enough.
I hope that I have been the child
      you always wanted,
because you are the mother
I will always love.

— Antony Simpson

Because of You...

I've known a mother's love.
I've sensed a mother's warm concern,
and I've been on the receiving end
    of a mother's friendship.
Because of you, I've been influenced
by someone I look up to with
    deep respect and total admiration.
You've always let me know that you
    care for me in the greatest way,
because you've given me a mother's love.

Today, I'm letting you know something
    I hope you've always been aware of:
    You mean the world to me,
    and you always will.
    Thank you for offering me
    a mother's love.
    I love you very much.

~ Barbara J. Hall

Mom, I'm working hard to build
the kind of life you raised me to believe in;
I'm following some dreams
that have always mattered to me.
The more I do, the more I realize how much
I'm using what you taught me about the world.
You deserve a world of thanks
    for everything you've given me:
courage to take chances (even to fail),
confidence to expect the best of myself,
and a profound sense of the joy that can
    be found in every day.
For all this and more,
I want to dedicate to you today the greatest
    goal I could ever achieve in my life:
        to make you proud of me.

~ Edmund O'Neill

Your Love Will Live Forever Within Me

You gave me life, nurtured and cared for me, and when you felt the time was right, you set me free. Through the years, never once did you complain or wish for things to be any different. You simply took your life in stride, no questions asked, embracing the happy moments along with the sad, accepting all things for what they were. That was your way.

I didn't always understand or appreciate everything you did. I was a child with my own innocent perception of the world. Now, as a grownup, I can reflect with such admiration and respect on the wonderful woman and mother you were then and still are today.

You stood with courage to meet the responsibilities that fell upon you and sacrificed so much for the love of your children. What you have accomplished is more than you will ever realize. When I think of all that you have done for our family and all the love you have so generously poured from your heart, I feel humbled. There will never be enough gratitude to offer to you or a means to repay you. But my heart will always be filled with the joy of knowing your love. It is the most precious gift I have ever received, for it is the one you have so wisely taught me to set free and share with others.

I love you for being a caring person, a remarkable woman, and an exceptional mother. Your love will forever live within me. Thank you for being my mother.

~ debbie peddle

Though We've Had Our Disagreements, I'll Always Love You, Mom

I know we haven't always
seen eye to eye, but that's okay.
Through all the happy moments
as well as the difficult ones,
I've always thought that you
were a good mother who wanted
what was best for me.
I know there have been times
when we had some problems communicating.
I haven't always agreed with everything
  you said and did,
but I'm realizing now that
  you're more than just my mother.

You are an individual,
  unique in your own way –
a woman with your own feelings, hopes,
  and dreams.

Now that I'm older, I'm beginning
to understand what you went through.
I may not need you in the same ways
I did when I was a child,
but I still need your support,
occasional advice, and always your love.
No matter what happens,
you'll always be my mother
and I'll always be your child –
and together, I want us to always be friends.

                              – Penny D. Kaplan

Thank You, Mom

I want to apologize
for any problems
that I may have caused you
in the past
I am not
the easiest person
to live with
since I am so
independent and strong
but you can be sure
that though it possibly
didn't seem like it
your values and ideals
did pass on to me
and I carry them forward
in all that I do

You always were someone
stable, strong, giving and warm
an ideal person to look up to
This has given me the
strength to lead
my own life
according to my own standards
Your leadership and love
have enabled me to grow
into a very
happy person
and I think that is
what every mother wishes
for her child
Thank you

— Susan Polis Schutz

Wherever we go
and whatever we do,
let us live with this
remembrance in our hearts...
   that we are *family*.
What we give to one another
comes *full* circle.
May we always be
   the best of friends;
may we always be one another's
   rainbow on a cloudy day;
as we have been yesterday
and today to each other,
   may we be so blessed
      in all our tomorrows...
         over and over again...

For we are a *family*, and that means
   love that has no end.

                    ~ Collin McCarty

The love
of a family
is so uplifting

The warmth
of a family
is so comforting

The support
of a family
is so reassuring

The attitude
of a family
towards each other
molds one's
attitude forever
towards the world

~ Susan Polis Schutz

The Greatest Gift
You Have Ever Given Me...
Is Your Love

I've changed a lot throughout my life,
always learning a little more about myself
and the world around me.
The challenges were interesting
and sometimes overwhelming,
but I always believed in myself enough
to get me through the hard times.
One of the things
that I've come to know now,
after all those changes,
is that I never once doubted
whether you'd be there for me
if I needed you.
And there were many times
when I did need you,
and you were there.

When I was headstrong and defiant,
you watched me strive for my independence,
knowing life's lessons are best learned
through personal experience.
When I was self ~ centered,
you watched me discover on my own
a broader outlook on life.
I came to understand life on my own terms
and to appreciate you even more
for the examples you set
and the lifestyle you've lived.
Having your unconditional love in my life
has made me feel secure and loved,
and that is the greatest gift
any parent could ever give.

~ Dena DiIaconi

Precious Mother, Sweetest Friend

When I'm about to give up, I think of you and I find the will to keep trying. When I feel unloved, I need only remember all you've done for me, and I am touched again by your example. When I need a friend, I know there's someone who loves me and will accept me with loving arms no matter what.

Your life is a testament to love. I know now that there were times when you sacrificed your time, your energy, and maybe even your dreams just so you could give to me, and your unselfishness still amazes me. Even when I wasn't sensitive to your own needs and I acted less than perfect, you always gave so much. The example of your life reveals the most loving heart and the sweetest kind of friendship, unlike any other I've ever known.

If these feelings could paint a picture, everyone could see that I have the most precious mother in all the world and the sweetest friend.

— Donna Fargo

I Love You Forever, Mom

You have shown me how to give of myself
You have shown me leadership
You have taught me to be strong
You have taught me the importance of the family
You have demonstrated unconditional love
You have demonstrated a sensitivity to people's needs
You have handed down to me the important
    values in life
You have handed down to me the idea of
    achieving one's goals
You have set an example, throughout your life
of what a mother and woman should be like
I am so proud of you
and I love you
forever

— Susan Polis Schutz

A Mother Is...

A mother is life at its best. She understands. She goes a million miles out of her way just to lend a hand. She brings you smiles when a smile is exactly what you needed. She listens, and she hears what is said in the spaces between the words. A mother cares, and she lets you know you're in her prayers.

A mother can guide you, inspire you, comfort you, and light up your life. A mother understands your moods and nurtures your needs. She lovingly knows just what would help make things right.

A mother always knows the perfect thing to do. She can make your whole day just by saying something that no one else could have said. Sometimes you feel like the two of you share a secret language that others can't tune in to.

When your feelings come from deep inside and need to be spoken to someone you don't have to hide from, you share them with your mother. When good news comes, she is the first one you turn to. When feelings overflow and tears need to fall, a mother helps you through it all.

A mother brings sunlight into your life. She warms your life with her presence, whether she is far away or close by your side. A mother is the most wonderful gift that brings happiness, and a treasure that money can't buy.

~ Collin McCarty

My Mother

For as long as I can remember
she has been by my side
to give me support
to give me confidence
to give me help

For as long as I can remember
she has always been the person
    I looked up to
so strong
so sensitive
so pretty

For as long as I can remember
and still today
she is everything a mother should be

For as long as I can remember
she has always provided stability
    within our family
full of laughter
full of tears
full of love

So much of what I have become
is because of you
and I want you to know
that I appreciate you, thank you
and love you
more than words can express

— Susan Polis Schutz

You Are Such a Wonderful Mother!

I want you to know how amazing you are: how much you're treasured and celebrated and quietly thanked.

I want you to feel really good... about all the great things you do! I want you to appreciate your uniqueness. Acknowledge your devotion and dedication. Realize what a beautiful soul you have. Understand the wonder within.

You make so much sun shine through, and you inspire so much gratitude in the lives of everyone who is lucky enough to be a part of that joy.

You are a very special person, giving so many people a reason to smile. You deserve to receive the best in return, and one of my heart's favorite hopes is that the happiness you give away will come back to warm you...
each and every day of your life.

— Sydney Nealson

To the Best Mother of All...
My Mom

If I had to pick one thing about you, Mom, that makes you so special, I don't think it would be possible.

I couldn't begin to count the number of times you tolerated my moods, consoled my heartbreaks and disappointments, endured my ups and downs, listened to words confused by tears, and just simply understood for no other reason than because you love me.

The years hold precious memories, but most of all, they hold growth. In a way, we grew up together. There's still some growing left to do, but one thing becomes more clear to me with each passing day, and I hope you know: there's no other mom like you, and I love you very much.

~ Susan M. Pavlis

In You, Mom, I've Seen Everything That Love Can Be

I've seen tears in your eyes ~ tears for my suffering, my happiness, and my disappointments. I've seen hope on your face ~ hope for my wishes, my blessings, and my best.

I've seen anger on your face, too ~ when you felt that someone was treating me unfairly, or when I was using bad judgment and you knew that I was hurting myself. I've seen joy in your eyes ~ when I reached for the stars and caught the moon, stars and all!

I've seen enthusiasm in you ~ when I was feeling inspired, self~assured, and certain that I could do anything I set out to do.

I've seen disappointment in you — when I tried but didn't achieve the thing I had set out to do, or when I lost something special to me and there was no way to help.

I've seen determination in you — when you wanted to be sure that I was happy. Whatever it might have cost you, I believe that you would have offered it gladly if you had to sacrifice it for my happiness.

I've seen strength in you — when I needed you to help me. I've felt the joy of your acceptance and understanding. I've known the warmth and comfort of having you there — always willing to give whatever I needed from you.

I've seen so much love in you — a love that is unconditional. Thank you, Mom. I love you, too.

— Regina Hill

ACKNOWLEDGMENTS

The following is a partial list of authors whom the publisher especially wishes to thank for permission to reprint their works.

Susan Hickman Sater for "When I Look at You, I See a Mother's Love and So Much More." Copyright © 2002 by Susan Hickman Sater. All rights reserved.

PrimaDonna Entertainment Corp. for "Thank You, Mother" and "Precious Mother, Sweetest Friend" by Donna Fargo. Copyright © 1996, 2001 by PrimaDonna Entertainment Corp. All rights reserved.

Regina Hill for "I Don't Know What I'd Do Without You." Copyright © 2002 by Regina Hill. All rights reserved.

T. L. Nash for "What Is a Mother's Love?" Copyright © 2002 by T. L. Nash. All rights reserved.

Barbara J. Hall for "It Takes Someone Special — Just like You — to Raise a Child." Copyright © 2002 by Barbara J. Hall. All rights reserved.

Kari Kampakis for "You Have Made Me into the Person I Am Today." Copyright © 2002 by Kari Kampakis. All rights reserved.

A careful effort has been made to trace the ownership of poems used in this anthology in order to obtain permission to reprint copyrighted materials and give proper credit to the copyright owners. If any error or omission has occurred, it is completely inadvertent, and we would like to make corrections in future editions provided that written notification is made to the publisher:

BLUE MOUNTAIN ARTS, INC., P.O. Box 4549, Boulder, Colorado 80306.